TIGERS
and Other Big Cats

Peter Gray

W

FRANKLIN WATTS
LONDON·SYDNEY

First published in 2013 by Franklin Watts

Copyright © 2013 Arcturus Publishing Limited

Franklin Watts
338 Euston Road
London NW1 3BH

Franklin Watts Australia
Level 17/207 Kent Street, Sydney NSW 2000

Produced by Arcturus Publishing Limited,
26/27 Bickels Yard, 151–153 Bermondsey Street, London SE1 3HA

The right of Peter Gray to be identified as the author of this work has been asserted by him in accordance with the Copyright, Designs and Patents Act 1988.

Illustrations: © Peter Gray
Editors: Joe Harris and Nicola Barber
Design: sprout.uk.com
Cover design: sprout.uk.com

A CIP catalogue record for this book is available from the British Library.

Dewey Decimal Classification Number 743.6'9755

ISBN 978 1 4451 1877 2

Printed in China

Franklin Watts is a division of Hachette Children's Books, an Hachette UK company.
www.hachette.co.uk

SL002690EN
Supplier 03, Date 0513, Print Run 2389

CONTENTS

DRAWING

In the early stages of a drawing you need to build up the general shape of your subject. These marks are called guidelines.

I have drawn the guidelines quite heavily to make them easy to follow, but you should work faintly with a hard pencil.

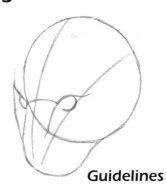

Guidelines

Use a softer pencil to develop the character and details. You may find that you do not follow the guidelines exactly in places. That's fine – they are only a rough guide.

Detail

Carefully erase the guidelines and mistakes. Then add shading and texture with a soft pencil.

Shading and texture

INKING

For a bold look go over the outlines with ink. Wait for the ink to dry thoroughly, then erase all the pencil marks.

Felt-tip pen outlines

The easiest inking method is to use a felt-tip pen. If you plan to add paint at a later stage, make sure your pen is waterproof or the paint will run.

For a more graceful effect, use a fine-tipped watercolour brush dipped in ink.

Brush outlines

COLOURING

Although I use watercolours in this book, the main principles are the same for any materials – start with the shading, then add in markings and textures, and finally work your main colours over the top.

Felt-tip colouring

Felt-tip pens produce bright, vibrant colours. Work quickly to avoid the pen strokes remaining visible.

Coloured pencils

Coloured pencils are the easiest colouring tools to use, but you have to take great care to blend the colours to achieve a good finish.

Watercolours

The subtlest effects can be achieved with watercolour paints. It is best to buy watercolour paints as a set of solid blocks that you wet with a brush. Mix the colours in a palette or on an old white plate.

TIPS AND TRICKS

HEADS AND FACES

To draw the face of any cat, try thinking of it as an upside-down triangle with a rough circle for the head and fur.

Basic shape

Cougar head

The circle is obvious in the rounded head of a cougar. All of the cougar's features fit within the triangle except for its **muzzle**.

The pattern is very similar for all of the cats. Only the **proportions** are different.

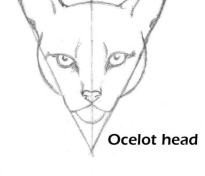

Ocelot head

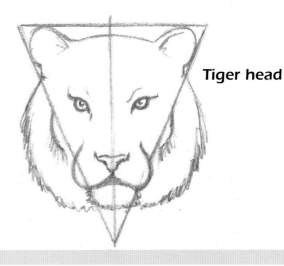

Tiger head

TIGER SKULL

It is useful for artists to have a basic understanding of what lies beneath the surface of the creatures they draw.

The tiger's skull reveals the awesome size of its teeth.

Tiger skull

When the tiger's face is drawn over the top of the skull, you can see that the main features (mouth, nose and eyes) are in quite a small central area.

TIGER SNARL

Try covering either side of this diagram with your hand to see two very different expressions.

When snarling, the tiger's lips curl back to reveal those great teeth. The rest of the face changes too – the eyes narrow, the bridge of the nose creases in deep wrinkles, and the ears flatten back against the head. Even the whiskers point up sharply.

Tiger snarl

CAT SKELETONS

Let's look at how the skeleton of a big cat compares to that of a pet cat.

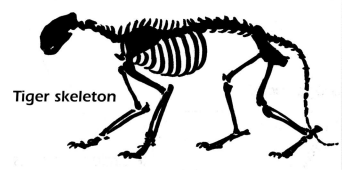

Tiger skeleton

The tiger has large shoulder blades, and a hump of spine at the shoulders. Its skull is surprisingly small, meaning that much of the head is actually made up of fur.

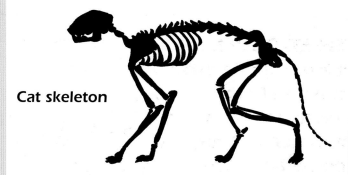

Cat skeleton

The basic body form of the pet cat is remarkably similar to that of the tiger. It is the proportions that are different – the tiger has a longer neck and shorter legs in relation to its overall shape.

TIGER

The largest of the big cats, the tiger is a strong and ferocious hunter. Its beautiful striped coat makes it difficult to spot in the grasslands and forests that are its home.

1 Although the tiger is a strong and thick-set animal, its body shape is in fact quite slender. Begin with a long oval and make it bow slightly in the middle. Mark a neat circle at the front end for the basic head shape.

2 Draw curving lines around the head to mark the centre of the face and the level of the eyes. Add in the lines of the powerful upper legs.

3 Develop the face by drawing guidelines for the muzzle, including a centre line running through both the upper and lower jaws. Extend the legs with the more angular shapes of the ankles and add some contours on the top edge to indicate the curve of the neck and protruding shoulders.

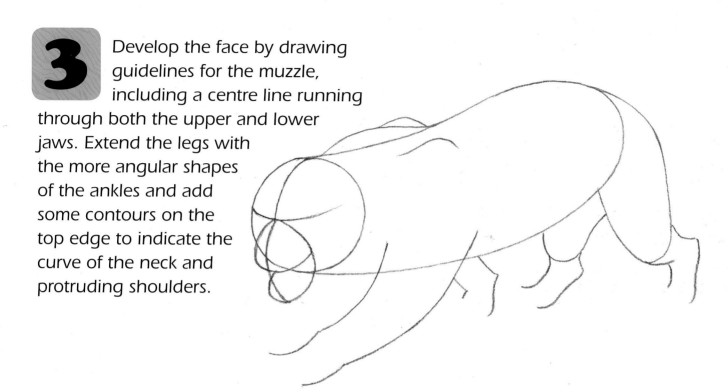

4 Copy the main features of the tiger's face, not forgetting the distinctive fur **ruff** around its jaw line. Add the toes, making sure they overlap each other convincingly. Then give your tiger a long, elegant tail.

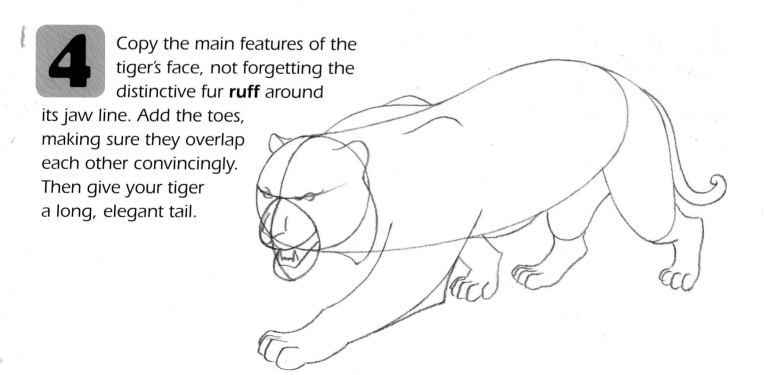

5 With the guidelines all established you can now enjoy working on the fine detail. Switch to a softer pencil and make sure it is sharp. Include a centre line down the tiger's back and some rough guidelines for the curves and spacings of the stripes.

6 For the inking stage, keep the outlines smooth and simple, allowing the brush to vary the weight of the lines. Use the tip of the brush, lightly loaded, to ink the eyes, mouth and nose. The black claws can be inked with single strokes. Don't erase the guidelines yet, as you will need them for the markings.

7 The tiger's markings are black stripes, so I have done them in ink. Work either side of the centre guidelines down the tiger's back and head to make the stripes symmetrical, and give them a rough, hairy texture. Don't do too many – leave some space in between each stripe.

COOL CATS

Unlike many cats, tigers love water. In the heat of the day, tigers often choose to cool off by taking a dip in lakes or streams. With their powerful bodies and webbed paws, tigers are strong swimmers. They can cover many kilometres in the water, crossing rivers or chasing prey.

ANIMAL FACTS

8 With your watercolours, mix up some watery grey using dark blue, red and maybe a touch of brown. Be sure you have decided the direction of the light – here it is coming from the upper right. Then apply some shading to the parts facing away from the light.

9 Mix some red and brown to make orange and paint the upper back, face and shoulders. Once it is dry, use an orangey brown to paint across the entire coloured area, which will blend the darker orange with the new colour. Remember to leave white patches on the face, belly and tail.

10 To finish the painting, add patches of colour to the eyes and mouth. Then put in any extra shading or richer colour that seems necessary. Use a fine brush and white ink to paint delicate **highlights** around the teeth, nose and ears and to add some very fine whiskers.

LION

The lion is king of the animals, with powerful legs for chasing prey. The male lion has a thick mane of hair around his neck. This bushy mane makes the lion look larger, which helps to frighten off rivals. The mane also protects the lion's neck during fights.

1 Start with the lion's head by drawing a triangle, point downwards. Position the triangle to the right of the page. Then draw a long egg shape, almost touching it. Leave enough space around the shapes to fit the rest of the lion on your paper. Look at the example to make sure your shapes are the right sizes in relation to each other.

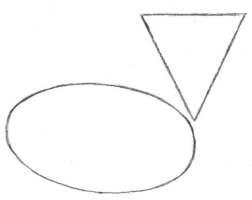

2 Next, you can add the strong upper parts of the lion's legs. Draw four long ovals, being careful to pay attention to the sizes and how they fit onto the body. You can then join up the chest and the hips with curved lines.

HUNTERS

Many lions live in groups called prides.
While the male lions protect the pride's territory,
it is the lionesses (female lions) that do most
of the hunting for food. They are smaller and
more agile than the males, and they often work
together to kill their prey.

ANIMAL FACTS

3 Complete the basic
lion shape with the
powerful lower legs
and the tail. Draw in a rough
outline for the mane. Mark
a centre line down the
lion's head, and a line
across at the level
of the eyes.

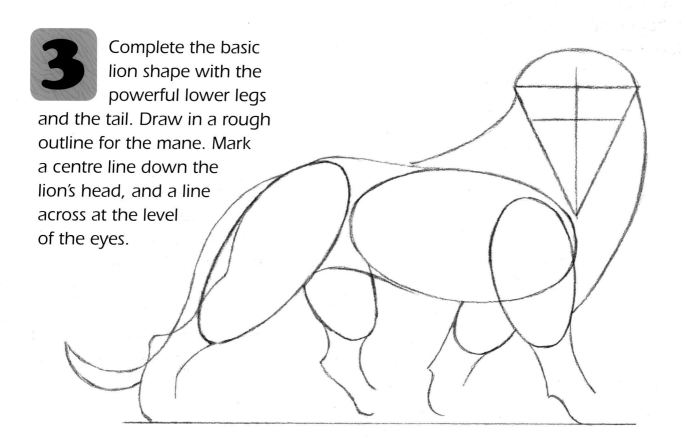

4 Continue to work on the lion's face. Use the guidelines to make sure the mouth, nose and eyes are symmetrical. Then draw the ears and add some texture to the outline of the mane. Draw the feet as individual rounded toes.

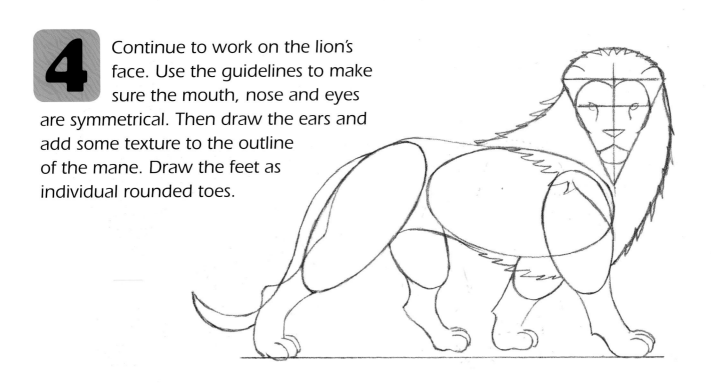

5 Now the basic lion shape is complete, you can start to look at the details. At this stage it's a good idea to work some texture into the mane to guide your ink drawing. You can also plan where the shading will appear on the lion's body.

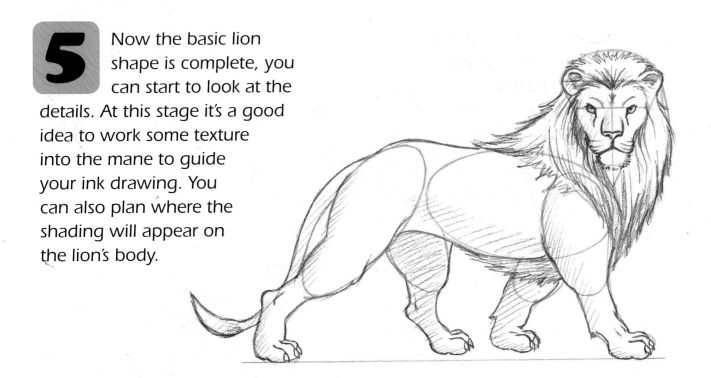

6 Apart from the mane, the lion has a smooth coat. Use black ink to create a smooth and graceful outline that brings out the animal's muscular build. The mane has a scruffier texture. Ink in the texture but don't overdo it – leave some space for the colour.

7 You might think a lion is the same sandy colour all over, but in fact its coat is darker and more orange across its back and on its tail and nose. The mane is also darker and slightly redder.

CHEETAH

The cheetah is the sprinter of the big cats. Its powerful, slender body is designed for rapid acceleration as the cheetah chases its prey. It uses its long tail for balance as it runs.

1 Three circles form the basic masses of the cheetah – the head, chest and hips. Take care over their relative sizes and the spaces in between, and notice that they do not sit level with each other, for this animal is in motion.

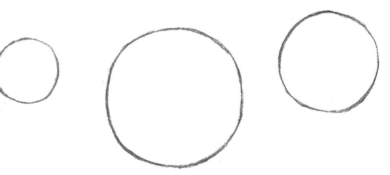

2 Join up the circles with a continuous, wavy line to form the neck and back, and extend it for the long tail. Mark the upper legs.

3 Now join up the lower parts of the circles and add the slender shapes of the lower legs and feet on the near side.

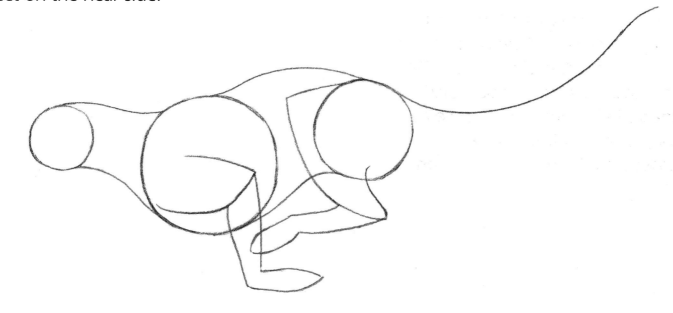

4 Add a muzzle and other head details and complete the tail. Draw in the legs on the far side, behind the limbs you've already put in.

5 Now there's not too much work to do to complete this profile. Refine the outline as necessary and plan your shading on the undersides if you find it helpful.

FAST CATS

The cheetah is the fastest animal on land. Its long legs and streamlined body make it the perfect sprinter over short distances. In bursts of speed it can accelerate to over 100 kilometres per hour (62 mph) across the African plains. At its fastest, the cheetah takes just over three strides per second!

ANIMAL FACTS

6 Inking the outlines requires a combination of sleek contours and some slightly ruffled, hairy texture around the shoulders, chest and tail. The markings should be small around the face, then larger and evenly spaced across the body. On the tail the markings are heavier, ending in rings.

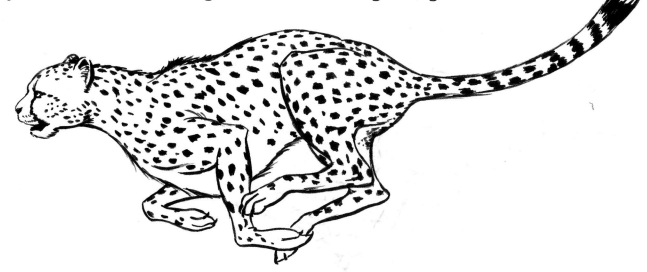

7 The cheetah is a rich sandy colour, a little darker across the shoulders and on the paws. The underside is white, with some shading. The addition of a patch of grass beneath the animal shows it to be off the ground and increases the sense of movement.

JAGUAR

The jaguar is the largest cat in Central and South America. It is a swift and agile hunter with a very powerful bite. Its name means 'one that kills with one leap'.

1 Start with a circle for the jaguar's head. The oval of the body has a shallow curve running up the back and a deeper curve to follow the more rounded tummy.

2 Start the rear end by extending the curve of the back around the **rump** and into the rear thigh. The front leg should be drawn right up into the shoulder and arched over the back. The guidelines should already have a solid, cat-like form.

3 Now add the foot shapes and tail. Then draw a centre line that wraps around the head, neck, shoulders and back.

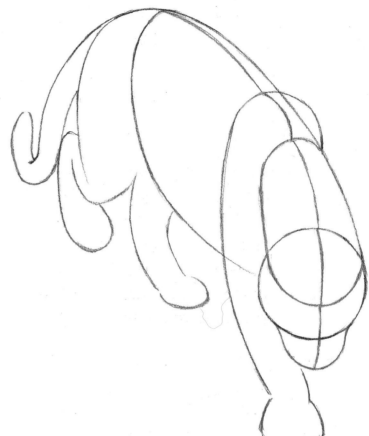

4 Draw in the main features of the head, working on either side of the centre line for symmetry. The toes should be strong and well-rounded. Add some curves around the tail to make it look rounded too.

5 Refine the drawing by adding more detail to the features, including the claws. A little shading will really help at the next stage. The downward motion of this pose requires a surface for the jaguar to be walking on. I've chosen a broad tree branch, but you could place your jaguar on rocks or rough ground.

6 At the inking stage, the real challenge is to put in the markings. Start at the head by adding small spots, mirrored on either side of the centre line. Make the spots larger as you work over the shoulders and back. Allow the markings to follow the curves across the body, getting slimmer around the shoulder, tummy and rump.

CLIMBING CATS

The jaguar stalks its prey before attacking with one deadly pounce. Jaguars are good at climbing trees and they are also excellent swimmers.

ANIMAL FACTS

7 The jaguar's colouring is quite simple – just a little richer across the top of the head, inside the ring markings and around the rear end. Leave the paws and lower face pale. Then concentrate on making the ground surface look natural. Some highlights may be helpful here.

JUNGLE SCENE

Learning how to draw and paint animals is just a step along the way to making finished pictures. A bigger challenge is to set your animals against a background that brings out their natural behaviour. Here are some of the steps I took to create a scene for the jaguar. You may choose to work with a different cat, or on a less complicated background.

1 After trying out many different **compositions** very roughly, I decided on this one and drew it quickly on scrap paper. The aim is to work out how the parts of the scene fit together, and be able to make alterations without messing up a detailed drawing.

2 Working on top of my rough pencil drawing, I added some shade and colour in broad blocks of watercolour. This helped me to see how the composition works.

3 Using black and white inks, I developed the lights and darks of the scene. I decided to make the foreground tree largely dark, showing in **silhouette** against the background. The ruined building is lighter against the darker background. I also decided to add another toucan.

4 On a larger sheet of heavier paper, start your artwork by drafting the main shapes and guidelines. The important principle here is to work broadly without any details at this stage.

5 Gradually develop the details, bringing form to the rough masses. Although I intended the building to be a ruin, I drew it as a complete shape first so that it would look convincing.

6 Use a softer pencil to complete the detailed drawing. Erase your guidelines as you go. I have left some of the detail sketchy, allowing some possibility for development in the ink and colour stages.

7 As I inked in the various lines and textures I decided that the main tree shape wasn't quite right, so I added another branch. When inking, it's important to keep in mind the light source and shading, and to add the appropriate texture to each surface.

8 Because I had worked out most of the light and shade decisions with my coloured rough (stage 2), I could apply the shading and colours to my ink drawing with confidence. A few highlights helped to bring out the details of the various plants.

GLOSSARY

composition The arrangement of the different parts of a picture.

highlight A bright area in a painting or drawing.

muzzle The nose and mouth of an animal such as a cat or dog.

proportion The size of one thing in relation to another.

ruff A ring of fur around the neck of an animal.

rump The back part of the body of an animal.

silhouette A dark shape visible against a brighter background.

WEBSITES

http://animals.nationalgeographic.co.uk/animals/big-cats/
Fascinating facts about big cats.

http://www.bbc.co.uk/nature/life/Felidae
Information, pictures and video clips about big cats from the BBC's archive.

FURTHER READING

Drawing Animals by Anna Milbourne (Usborne Publishing, 2009)

Explore and Draw Big Cats by Monica Halpern (Rourke Publishing, 2010)

How to Draw Animals by Michael Garton (Buster Books, 2010)

How to Draw Big Cats by Carolyn Franklin (Book House, 2006)

INDEX